Prison Segmentation For Your Rehabilitation

R U Ready?

Reverend Mike Wanner

Copyright

October 11, 2017

Reverend Mike Wanner

Selected Images Used by License

Table Of Contents

Table Of Contents 3
Introduction 4
1 - I am Writing This Book Because 5
2 - Prison Complexity 7
3 - How Can Prisoners Cope With What Is? 11
4 - The Reality of Now 12
5 - Prison Staff 15
6 - Prisoner's Needs 17
7 - Prisons Are A Bit Of A Mess 19
8 - Aligning With A Higher Purpose 20
9 - Segmentation For Rehabilitation 22
10 - Prisoners Reconnections Needed? 23
11 - Initial Program Blocks 24
12 - The Future Can Be Optimal 25
13 - Thank You 26
14 - Don't Worry Ever 27
15 - Resource Books 28
16 - Angels Please Prayers 30
17 - Private Channeling 31
18 - Reverend Mike Wanner 32

Introduction

Are You The One This Book Is For?

I write with the idea of being helpful to the children of God who are incarcerated and their families.

Sources report that in America alone there are more than 2.3 million people in prison or jail. Their incarceration further complicates the lives of those who are their children.

Spouses are another large group of people who are impacted.

Parents are another large group of people who are impacted.

Siblings are another large group of people who are impacted.

The topic of segmentation that I introduced in my last few books can be the crucial piece of the puzzle of what to do about the prison mess.

Millions Are Hurting

Time To Reassess

Eliminate Collateral Damage

Cooperate

1 - I am Writing This Book Because

In 2013, Angel Raphael invited me to visit a prison energetically. While delayed by other books, The invitation was honored in 2016, and that led to publishing the following books related to prisons:

1. *Angel Raphael Speaks Volume 4: Angels, Addicts, Alcoholics & Prisoners - Oh Yeah!*
2. *Angel Raphael Speaks Volume 5: Prisoners Caring for Alcoholics - Australia In Miniature   Projects Intro*
3. *Angel Raphael Speaks Volume 6: Prisoners Caring for Addicts - Australia In Miniature For   Addicts*
4. *Prison Jobs Now: Providing Care For Addicts And Alcoholics*
5. *Angel Raphael Speaks - Prisons (A Kindle only book -2013)*
6. *Contained Care Communities: Concept*
7. *Australia In Miniature*
8. *Prison Possibilities Dialogue Series: Concept*
9. *Prison Possibilities Dialogue Series: Volume 2 Dialogues*
10. *Prison Possibilities Dialogue Series: Volume 3 Dialogues*
11. *Prison Possibilities Dialogue Series: Volume 4 Dialogues*
12. *Prison Possibilities Dialogue Series: Volume 5 Dialogues*
13. *Prison Possibilities Voluntary Exile: Concept*
14. *Prison Possibilities Correction Coaches: Concept*
15. *Prison Possibilities for Mexicans: Is A Boat Better than A Wall?*
16. *Prison Possibilities Family Time: A Reason to Thrive!*
17. *Prison Genius Pool: "So Much Genius In Jail."*
18. *Prison Possibilities Access Systems: Prisoner Access by Request*
19. *Prisoner's Lawyers Can Save The American Economy: Make A Buck Doing It & Be Thanked!*
20. *Prisoner Family Talks, Days, Stays & Vacations: Connecting Helps Healing*
21. *Prisoner Writing Projects: Write To Heal, Start Over & Reconnect*
22. *Prison Cell Clearing & Blessing: Clear Entities, Chase Ghosts, and & Create Sacred Space*
23. *Prisoner Professors: Show You Are Aware Create Change With Care*

24. *Prison Reiki? Maybe Someday? A Gateway To Help Heal Prisons & America?*
25. *Judges and An Angel Rule On Possibilities: We Can Cut Sentences & Prison Costs*
26. *Ideas For Prison Wardens: Leadership Is Not Easy*
27. *Solitary Community: Could Community Support Cut Costs and Issues?*
28. *Prisoner Projects Communication Teams: Communications Can Change Lives*
29. *Motivating & Empowering Prisoners? Invite Prisoners To Find Their Motivation & Their Future*
30. *Prison Segmentation for Safety*
31. *Prison Segmentation for Security*
32. *Dowsing For Prisoners*
33. *Ex-Prisoners Possibilities with Real Estate Investors*
34. *Prison Segmentation For Mental Peace*
35. *Prison Segmentation For Joint Ventures*
36. *Prison Segmentation For Startups Ideas*

This book continues to carry the potential for rethinking that can help to reduce incarceration to those who we need to have there.

I want to trigger mindset shifts in the prisoners as well as employees and the community. We need a lot more Objective Productive Dialogues about Enhancing the lives of Prison Employees, Prisoners, Taxpayers and the Families of all.

2 - Prison Complexity

The prison situation is complicated by political waffling on what is in the news, and all this has evolved into quite a mess. It now seems that change is almost impossible because of the human dynamics of overwhelm that make everything so complicated.

Libraries insist on silence because minds are at work. Users need to be able to hear themselves think.

Thinking is good, and all my books invite thinking and measured rethinking of what is going on in prison. I have no ax to sharpen and have no intention of attacking anybody's position.

Many of the significant issues have been made in the distant past and focusing on them is a tremendous waste of time and energy.

Unfortunately, Incarceration is very complicated because there are many changes needed and the present thinking is confrontational without results. Fighting authority and organizational concept development is not productive and a poor use of everybody's time. Teamwork and diligence are the answers we need to pursue.

Defensiveness can save some damage to some reputations, but better would be to develop new reputations of teamwork, development, and integration. We need to work together and create new options for everyone.

The Mass incarceration of recent years has made a complicated situation worse, and the tragic circumstance of our country continue to compound the complex nature of the consequences.

There seems to be little good news about prisons and lots of reports of the rigidity that continues and even increases isolation from family. Denial of rights is alleged, contaminated food is alleged, so-called inadequate health care of prisoners, poor treatment of women prisoners is claimed, and it continues to round up to a large number of prisoner abuse allegations that can contribute to further negative consequences as it seems that defensiveness is the only way to protect everybody from everybody.

The books that I referenced above present a lot of ideas about moving forward in a collaborative way but there is one significant obstacle, and that is space. The segmentation concept can be helpful in spreading out the people to allow a little more space so that there can hopefully be some more opportunity for realignments.

I would encourage every reader to begin to think about segmentation as the key to collaboration which can be the goal that can serve everybody. Giving negativity and receiving negativity have a poisonous sting that can be hurtful to a lot of people for a long time.

Conversations that lead to collaborations can be instrumental in improving things, but the real challenge is to eliminate the emotional delivery of blaming which can create an explosive façade of needing to be tough and that toughness can be a seeming macho trap.

Consider if you were still in high school and let's use some stereotypical players to represent the obstruction dynamics of some personality types.

The big macho dude who the girls think is fantastic can be the hero to a lot of guys. The same gentlemen may not be as appealing to the girls once they get to know him as his roughness can be turn off if he starts to push the girls in ways that are not satisfactory.

If the women begin to turn against a guy, then the guys may not have the same level of respect because he is seen as less of a leader in the male/female dynamics that other guys respected so much.

Now that is an oversimplification of the dynamics, but there is a balance point lesson to all of this. The point is about a balance between macho and maturity.

In prison, there is also a balance between macho and maturity and the values are different as are the players. In jail, there is an absence of the feminine dynamic which makes the situation different and even more stressful as the pull to win the hand of a fair maiden is not in the near term.

The human need for recognition and identification is still a challenge that the prisoner feels, but the path forward can have many contradictions which can leave the prisoners at a loss for what to do, feel and act. In High School, popularity was relatively comfortable, and the path was clear.

Prison may have less opportunity, but still, there can be a tendency to push for popularity and respect. There may be an opportunity to have alone time where you can stop and think about recreating yourself into a person that you might like just fine.

If you made mistakes, be kind to yourself. If you made huge mistakes, be even more compassionate to yourself.

Yesterday is history. You can make a new chapter to a whole new book of all your possibilities.

Do not expect the way forward to be easy but start the journey anyhow. The first person you need to convince and impress if yourself.

If you have no confidence, why should anyone else? Take the time, prepare your steps and begin anew on the path to the new You.

It is not likely that the complexity of prison will change soon. I do not expect a revolutionary climate to evolve anytime soon, but I pray that you do not wait because the bus could leave without you if you are not ready with a ticket you wrote for yourself.

3 - How Can You Cope With What Is?

Left to the ordinary prison dynamics constituencies, the answer to the title of this chapter is to continue as best as you have been able.

An alternative may develop if the other books that I have written on segmentation are embraced by the authorities. Another hope may be an initiative from within you that declares ideas that may offer hope, economy, cooperation and reasonable alternatives.

Prisons, Prisoners, Taxpayers, prison staff and their families and all connected to all of them are very important as they are losing at every step of the existing system and their families suffer because resources spent in prison are not available to the government to spend on the people outside the walls.

Prisoners can have a choice hopefully to choose between the way things are and the way things could be if there is a definite demonstration of cooperative effort to improve the lives of all who live, work or pay for incarceration.

As you read these ideas, please begin to develop your thinking so you will be able to decide whether to suffer the complicated situation that is or if you want to participate in the development of your prison home into a Renaissance reality.

4 - The Reality Now

From where I sit at home before the TV, the news for prisoners and their families keeps getting worse, and as that happens, there is a kind of double down which makes change even less likely. What is being done is not helpful for prisoners or their families.

Visitation gets more complicated and human contact less frequent. There seems to be little recognition that the direction of change is not helpful to anybody.

Change seems to be moving in the wrong direction, and the human connection does not seem to be recognized as the pivotal piece in rebuilding families and lives. There are a lot of complaints about the high level of recidivism, but the chain of exit help seems to have prominent links missing.

Moving away from a destination is not helpful to the completion of a journey. The system that seems broken also seems to have aggressive efforts towards moving further away from common sense.

The experts could make more optimal choices for success if they were available. Direction change is unlikely unless there is a groundswell of creativity for restructuring.

Prison riots are calling attention to the problem, but they are unlikely to add positivity for options. Hopefully, segmentation can offer some choices, some freedom, and some options.

Please consider developing negotiating skills and communication skills in a deliberate constructive reorganizational effort. With effort by everybody, hopefully, safety and quality of life can be improved.

Teamwork is lacking now, but it can be developed so that there is enough assertiveness to move forward but also enough to efficiently collaborate. Blaming anybody does not lay a foundation of teamwork that can be used again and again to progress in a positive win-win way.

While talking may seem counterproductive and frequently is, there is a lot of value and peace to be found in sharing your viewpoint and having those points be assembled into a comprehensive plan to reveal the message that can be a jewel to the settlement of long-standing issues.

Effective communication can lead to the respect which can lead to people changing their minds and their positions. I would encourage all prisoners to start developing teams that can document the reasonable ideas that can represent a consistent level of a request. Patience can serve all well now.

Once you have the ideas, you can search by your team to find an even-tempered person who can reformat your position into something that could be a little more manageable than what was first written.

It may seem that I have shifted the conversation from you to the community. The reason for that is each participant can contribute to the complexity or simplicity of the resolution.

Each person can also contribute to peace that pervades the premises. If you ever want to get out and find a good life, your efforts can help.

Even if you do not expect ever to get out again, you can be a positive influence on your remaining time and all who will be with you. When you change ever so slightly, so will the world.

5 - Prison Staff

Prison staff appreciates a safe environment in which to work. Prison staff could be influenced by prisoners if they will just evolve their interactions to help produce ongoing win-win collaborations about interactive intellectually driven goals.

Who is responding to whom and would anybody like to change? There is a teamwork effect needed between the prison staff and the prisoners that could seek enhanced understanding, teamwork, and shared goal-setting.

In human dynamics terms, isolation and desensitization block meaningful interaction, teamwork, and social acceptance. All humans are social beings, and this façade impedes the personal growth of both prisoners and corrections officers.

The isolation kills any seeds of kindness, and that hurts everybody. Kindness stifled before action does not circulate, and therefore no reciprocity occurs.

This situational walling off can be diminished over time for the betterment of all, but that is not likely to happen within the existing constraints of interaction.

Something is needed to protect the personalities and situations of both groups so there can be a safety zone of creative space for the cultivation of new interactive resources. Segmentation can create that safe possibility, but that will only be possible if the process begins.

Would it not be wonderful if prisoners and prison staff can morph into leaders who are open and interactive within the segmented areas of prisons that provide a new level of safety and interaction.

Resistance could evaporate when defensiveness transforms into questioning, evaluation and recompiled integrated plans.
In the theatre and movies, an actor can show every level of human potential in the same scene.

The role player's of the old prison scene needed to maintain a macho {Don't mess with me} image. That image may have seemed almost like a barrier that provided protection, but in reality, it was an obstruction to team building and teamwork. Segmentation can allow that to fade.

Prisoners in segmented arrangements could consider broadcasting their openness as a reasonable adult human being who can be worked with for the betterment of all.

The obstacle to connectivity has been prisoners need to defend themselves physically, mentally, emotionally and spiritually from attack. Those impediments can all be eliminated.

Let's close the history books and write some new chapters about progress with new freedoms.

6 - Prisoner's Needs

While this chapter title could be an unlimited book, I will start the discussion and expect the best. My approach is different than most that you will read as I endeavor to find the opportunity for reconnection.

There is a dynamic about prison that is applied judgment which has an impact of brand tarnishing. The convictions seem to act as a tag or label of toxicity that warns the world.

Over time the acceptance of the broader community ruling can have a prisoner accepting their label as permanent. Every brand can be revitalized if the owner can take the possibility and declare they are in the creation mode of a new self-image.

The most important attitude to change is one's own. Once you get there, others can feel the shift in you and the harmony that radiates from your soul and then they can judge the intensity of the peace and the power of the joy that you share.

Make no mistake, the effort to reinvent yourself will not be easy, but the decision to do so can be the critical difference between wishing and creating. This realignment will be no small thing and could take a lot of internal processing.

Imagine that this is the first step in creating a new you and it will be.

And what else would you like to work on? Polishing the diamond that you are is important for you to sparkle anew for yourself and everybody else. Fear not for self-work can be very satisfying. It also destroys the negativity that settles in when you leave things unresolved.

Throughout my life, I always struggled to understand whatever did not make sense to me. That has to lead me to a view of the uniqueness that we each have.

Individuality is a beautiful and powerful way to manifest one's personal power and presence in the world. Our own identity can then embrace or deflect the uniqueness of others.

Prisoners have more uniqueness to overcome issues than many others. You can use your individuality to select a strategic alliance which resonates with the perfect right people.

Developing your connections with others can change your life and all the potential that is available to you.

Prisoners also have vulnerabilities that need to be cautiously managed to avoid complications. Just because you have a breakthrough in your personal circumstances, does not mean that those weaknesses will disappear.

So, the prison could be a minefield that needs to be cautiously traveled for your safety. If you work on polishing what you are and have and do that is good, then the diamond you are can sparkle for all to see.

7 - Prisons Are A Bit Of A Mess

Earlier in this book I wrote, "The prison situation is complicated by political waffling on what is cool and exciting, and all this has evolved into quite a mess. It now seems that change is almost impossible because of the human dynamics of overwhelm that make everything so confused."

Just last night I heard the story on Sixty Minutes of an Associate Law Professor at Georgetown University who was previously incarcerated. A convicted bank robber is walking the streets again as a free citizen and being employed by a prestigious law school that teaches the lawyers for the next generation.

The contrast between those two Resume' items is quite remarkable. We live in America, and our nation is full of people with different experiences.

It is remarkable when people prevail in anything against all the odds. Whether surviving a car accident or an earthquake, the hand of God can be seen in many places at many times.

Things have not changed, but there are exceptions to the rules when diligent people set out to do courageous things and prove others wrong. We can do a lot if we try and I invite you to try.

The Angel Raphael Series that I channel clearing indicates the power that a prisoner can have when that have a purpose in mind.

8 - Aligning With A Higher Purpose

Angel Raphael in Message Set 10 had a lot to say about the importance of purpose to the life of a prisoner. Here it is:

"Prison Rehabilitation

The answer to prison rehabilitation is purpose. While some institutions may have initiated programs to engage their residents, the feeling of a purposeful life brings a new reality to the incarcerated.

Purposes for consideration will be ones that work for the incarcerated as well as the society which actually pays the bills. Unique characteristics to include would be the creation of a feeling of accomplishment generated by prisoner effort and drastic cost savings for the institution.

The real loss to prisons is wasted time, no productivity and no graciousness of interactive genius. If invited, the right use of time can provide different results than now seen.

There is no profit to society when cruelness is applied to the control of citizens. There may be temporary security, but that comes at a significant price to the potential of all.

The best way to learn about what is possible is to listen to the troubled stories of the incarcerated people. Their genius can be tapped by mining information about how to fill the gap that they slipped in to so that newer walkers on their path can find the void filled by their charity of sharing their pain as a love patch to the sinkholes of society.

The answers through this channel are coming differently than most could conceive and that is because neither you nor I have a job whose agenda has its own needs.

You ask to imagine how much can be cut from prison costs to maintain security, improve lives, create a new industry and improve the focus, flavor, and flair of American life and you dowsed for an answer. You got 47% reduction, and you questioned your dowsing. Your questioning is wise because there is a vast industry that has roots in the status quo.

While that is true, your answer has potential that will serve the ones that would resist the initiatives that flow from the message. Their positions are survivable as is for a time unknown but their openness to change can also serve their security.

The change will happen even if they choose to use their money to resist the inevitable avalanche of change. Their opportunities are paramount in the areas of personal safety for all and the possibility to create new meaningful arrangements that are self-sustaining for all levels of the resident base and those employed in the industry." ARS 10

9 - Segmentation For Rehabilitation

It seems that one of the significant obstructions to rehabilitation is the multitude of mindsets that spiral down all potentials. The mindsets seem to be rigidly in opposition to the success of the apparent thought thinker enemy.

The opposition seems to be to anybody and everybody that tries to bring forth a concept for consideration. We have had enough obstruction, thank you.

Let us no longer double down on obstruction to progress. Let us instead double up on listening and selecting things that we can agree upon as helpful.

Prisons are very full, and that adds complexity to efforts to rehabilitate prisoners. Everywhere there are people and no space.

Segmentation adds space, and that can help relaxation.

Relaxation can allow clear thinking.

Clear thinking can allow options.

Options allow empowerment.

Empowerment allows personal peace.

Personal peace allows planning.

Planning sets a person up to step forward and succeed.

10 - Prisoners Reconnections Needed?

Readers are invited to consider the connectivity they have with others both in and outside the walls.

We can do this if we try and I invite you to try. We need to know who would be willing to do what at your particular facility. This whole segmentation program would be optional and subject to a real strong desire to participate.

Those wanting to participate could have their skills be categorized broadly at first and then refined as we go along.

This information could be administratively segregated if that was deemed necessary. The reason for the data is to see what potential there could be to develop programs that would be helpful, entertaining, or educational to other prisoners.

Priority Interests would be to find expertise that could be tapped to offer valuable knowledge and training to residents. Skill owners that could be most helpful to help segmentation provide real opportunities are those who are:

    Experienced Teachers of Anything
    Credentialed Teachers
    Professional Certification Holders
    People with technical skills certifications
    Prisoners who have Administrative Skills
    Prisoners who have Administrative Management Skills
    Prisoners with manual skills
    Prisoners with hobby skills
    Prisoners with creativity

11 - Initial Program Blocks

I have already dropped some hints in other books of the segment blocks that I would like to see considered. The program initially can be a stress-busting relief system that can lower the tension level for all and improve the peace.

The program would need to develop so everybody could understand the participation behaviors that will give them the most options. Each facility could establish their own priorities.

You could decide if any of the following are good starting points:

        Two-hour program block
        Three-hour program block
        Four-hour program block
        Five-hour program block
        Six-hour program block
        Seven-hour program block
        One- night Segmentation
        Two-night Segmentation
        One-week Segmentations
        Writers Segmentations
        Efficiency Segmentations
        Security Segmentations
        Safety Segmentations
        Creativity Segmentations

12 - The Future Can Be Optimal

A significant consideration for all is the importance of taxpayers getting a break so they will have a reason to participate, authorize, support and recognize the efforts.

Segmentation can be started incrementally and built into a whole new life for so many people whereby prisoners can get out of jail sooner than later while the community safety is the same.

Good Things Can Still Happen:

Taxpayers can be charged less.
Children can get back with their parent/s.
Spouses can get their partners back.
Prisoners can find love again.
Parents can get their adult children back.
Brothers and sisters can get their siblings back.
Children can get their Aunts and Uncles back.
Prison staff can work in a safer environment.
Prisoners can have their time in prison be safer.
Prisoners can have their time in prison be more peaceful.
Lifers can have options that would not be otherwise available.
Recidivism can be reduced.

Prisons, Prison Staff, Prisoners, Taxpayers, and Communities can decide. Best wishes to all.

May all who read this be blessed AND SO IT IS!
Mike

13 - Thank You

For Considering These Ideas

14 - Don't Worry Ever

Ever

It Does Not Help Prayer Still Does!

Resource: http://www.Create-A-Prayer.com

15 - Resource Books

Distant Healing Sessions (or Join Mail List) – Write To mikewann@voicenet.com

Books by Rev. Mike at www.Amazon.com

Veterans Healing Six Pack
1. *Trauma Healing Options for VA Hospitals: Help for Veterans to Own Their Healing and their future.*
2. *Trauma Healing Action Steps for Veterans: Help to Start Healing*
3. *Trauma Healing Action Steps for Veterans: Empowerment*
4. *Trauma Healing Action Steps for Veterans: Forgiveness*
5. *Trauma Healing Action Steps for Veterans: Thought Freedom*
6. *Tea For Veterans: Welcome One Home*

PTSD Power Pack:
1. *The PTSD Project: Turn Pain To Power*
2. *PTSD & Soul Retrieval: Putting One Back Together*
3. *PTSD & The Purple PAD: Calling all Scientists and PTSD Patients*

Angel Raphael Speaks Volume 1: Take Courage! God Has Healing in Store for You!
Angel Raphael Speaks Volume 2: Take Courage! God Has Healing in Store for You!
Angel Raphael Speaks Volume 3: Take Courage! God Has Healing in Store for You!
Angel Raphael Speaks Volume 4: Angels, Addicts, Alcoholics & Prisoners – Oh Yeah!
Angel Raphael Speaks Volume 5: Prisoners Caring for Alcoholics - Australia In Miniature Projects Intro
Angel Raphael Speaks Volume 6: Prisoners Caring for Addicts - Australia In Miniature For Addicts
Reiki Journaling from Japan
Reiki Is Alive: God's Great Gift
Four Parts to Healing
Distant Healing: We Are All Connected
Stress Release Energy Work: How To Cope
Does Reiki Love Heal Cancer?
Group Consciousness
Salute To Philadelphia VA Medical Center: Thank You
Reiki Transcript for Reiki 2 & 3 Channels: Dr. Usui Is That You?
God Bless Kindle & Amazon
Puppies Are Different From People
If Your Dog Dies
Toy Guns Are Obsolete

Great Spirit Made Children With Red Skin: AND
The Cage of Fear: Is Not Locked
God Made Children Red, Yellow, Brown, Black & White: Greet Each Child With Kindness
Emergency Medical Kindness In The Cradle Of Liberty: Big City - Cracked Bell
Angels Are Always Around Addicts and Addicts: Help Is Near Now! Invite It In!
Angels Are Always Around Addicts and Alcoholics: Volume 2 - Tools To Help Re-Light Your Life
Prison Jobs Now: Providing Care For Addicts And Addicts
Controlled Care Communities Concept
Prison Possibilities Dialogue Series: Concept
Prison Possibilities Dialogue Series: Volume 2, 3, 4, 5 Dialogues
Prison Possibilities Voluntary Exile
Prison Possibilities Corrections Coaches
Prison Possibilities For Mexicans: Is A Boat Better Than A Wall?
Prison Possibilities Family Time: A Reason to Thrive!
Prison Genius Pool: "So Much Genius In Jail."
Prison Possibilities Access Control: Prisoner Access by Request
Prisoner's Lawyers Can Save The American Economy: Make A Buck Doing It & Be Thanked!
Prisoner Family Talks, Days, Stays & Vacations: Connecting Helps Healing
Prisoner Writing Projects: Write To Heal, Start Over & Reconnect
Prison Cell Clearing & Blessing: Clear Entities, Chase Ghosts, & Create Sacred Space
Prisoner Professors: Show You Are Aware Create Change With Care
Prison Reiki? Maybe Someday? A Gateway To Help Heal Prisons & America?
Judges and An Angel Rule On Possibilities: We Can Cut Sentences & Prison Costs
Ideas For Prison Wardens: Leadership Is Not Easy
Solitary Community: Could Community Support Cut Costs and Issues?
Prison Project Communications Team: Communications Can Change Lives
Motivating & Empowering Prisoners? Invite Prisoners To Find Their Motivation
Prison Segmentation For Safety, And Sanity, Security, Peace, and Space
Prison Segmentation For Security
Dowsing for Prisoners; Answers from Above
Ex-Prisoner Possibilities With Real Estate Investors
Prison Segmentation For Joint Ventures

Little Books at Kindle.com by Rev. Mike:
English Medical History Questionnaire For Non-English Speakers
English Language Helper For Non-English Speakers
Wise Wonderful Women Are The Well Of The Family
Answers for Test & Research: Dowsing Power
Crisis? Reiki! Baby? Reiki!
Bible References For Healing
Angel Raphael Speaks – Prisons
Angel Raphael Speaks – Veterans
The Saint Off Interstate 95

16 - Angels Please Prayers

Addict's

Angels of Healing Selected
Help Me to Stay Directed
Come To Me From The Sky
I Am Ready to Succeed Not Try
If I Don't Invite You In
I Might Not Win
I Have Been Lost For Too Long
Help Me To Stay Strong

Alcoholic's

Angels of Healing On High
Help Me to Stay Dry
Come To Me From The Sky
I Am Ready to Succeed Not Try
If I Don't Invite You In
I Might Not Win
I Have Been Lost For Too Long
Help Me To Stay Strong

From

http://AngelRaphaelSpeaks.com/AAAAAAA/

17 - Private Channeling

Angel Raphael Speaks a series of free messages that are channeled through Reverend Mike Wanner for the Highest good and Highest Healing of all concerned.

Many questions arise about Reverend Mike doing private channeling, and he does help with that so e-mail him.

Reverend Mike is available worldwide as a psychic channel, emotional release facilitator, spiritual energy practitioner & teacher, and public speaker. He looks forward to meeting you soon!

Email - mikewann@voicenet.com 215-342-1270 PRIVATE SPIRITUAL READINGS/channelings or Spiritual Healing Sessions: Telephone or in person. Rev. Mike is available for private, one-on-one intuitive sessions with you, his Guide Family, and your Guides. He helps by offering clarity on emotional situations about your life, your purpose, your spirituality, and the release of stuffed emotions and cellular memory.
Connect to the love of your Guides today!
Contact Rev. Mike for an appointment.

Sessions available:
Spiritual Readings
Angel Channeling
Distant Reiki Healing
Remote Clearing of Stuffed Emotions
Distant Clearing Cellular Memory
Distant Clearing Energy Blockages
Remote Clearing of the Chakras
Customized needs
Mastermind dowsing responses to yes/no direction finding questions.

Rev. Mike is a facilitator of healing. He brings you and the Divine together so that you can align with the Divine and have a great time and a great life. All healing is between you and God, as it should be. Go ahead and start without Rev. Mike. Visit his prayer site http://www.Create-A-Prayer.com. Take the first step NOW.

18 - Reverend Mike Wanner

Rev. Mike Wanner started his Metaphysical and Ministerial studies with Reiki in 1993 and had studied seven styles of Reiki in the U.S., Japan, Canada, Denmark and Australia. He is certified to teach. He became certified to teach Integrated Energy Therapy in 1999 and co-taught the first IET class of the new Millennium. Mike began dowsing in 2001.

Ordained as a Metaphysical Minister of the International Metaphysical Ministry and an Interfaith Minister of the Circle of Miracles Ministry, Rev. Mike practices and teaches spiritual energy therapies in the Philadelphia Area.

Rev. Mike holds ministerial degrees from the University of Metaphysics and the University of Sedona. He is a Pastoral Care Associate of Aria - Frankford Hospital. He taught at the National Academy of Massage Therapy and Health Sciences.

Rev. Mike was a faculty member of the Medical Mission Sister's Center for Human Integration's School of Integrated Body/Mind Therapies in Fox Chase, Philadelphia, PA for twelve years.

Rev. Mike is licensed by the teaching of Intuitional Metaphysics to practice Spiritual Healing and Scientific Prayer. Mike is also a Prayer therapist.

Rev. Mike was elected in 2007 to the status of "Fellow of the American Institute of Stress."

In 2008, Rev. Mike became a practitioner of Coincidental Recognition as he incorporated the CoRe System into his spiritual healing practice.

In 2009, Rev. Mike trademarked a new healing process called Quantum Quatro! Subtle Energy System Support®.

In 2011, Rev. Mike joined the outreach program known as the Health Advantage Group.

In 2012, Rev. Mike became a Certified Professional Coach by The Master Coaching Academy and Joined the Personal Empowerment Group.

Before his Metaphysical, Ministerial and Coaching studies, Rev. Mike worked for Sears Roebuck and Co. while in High School and after graduation, until he joined the U. S. Air Force in 1965. He returned to Sears from Vietnam in 1969 and stayed until 1978. His final Sears assignment was as an efficiency expert in Methods - Operational Research and Development.

He volunteered with Burholme Emergency Medical Services from 1969 and is still a Life Member and Board of Directors Member. He started a private ambulance company in 1975 and worked professionally in the field until 2001 when he devoted his full attention to real estate investing, healing, coaching, and writing.

May All Who Read This Be Blessed
AND SO IT IS!

www.ingramcontent.com/pod-product-compliance
Lightning Source LLC
Chambersburg PA
CBHW050035230526
45470CB00003B/1298